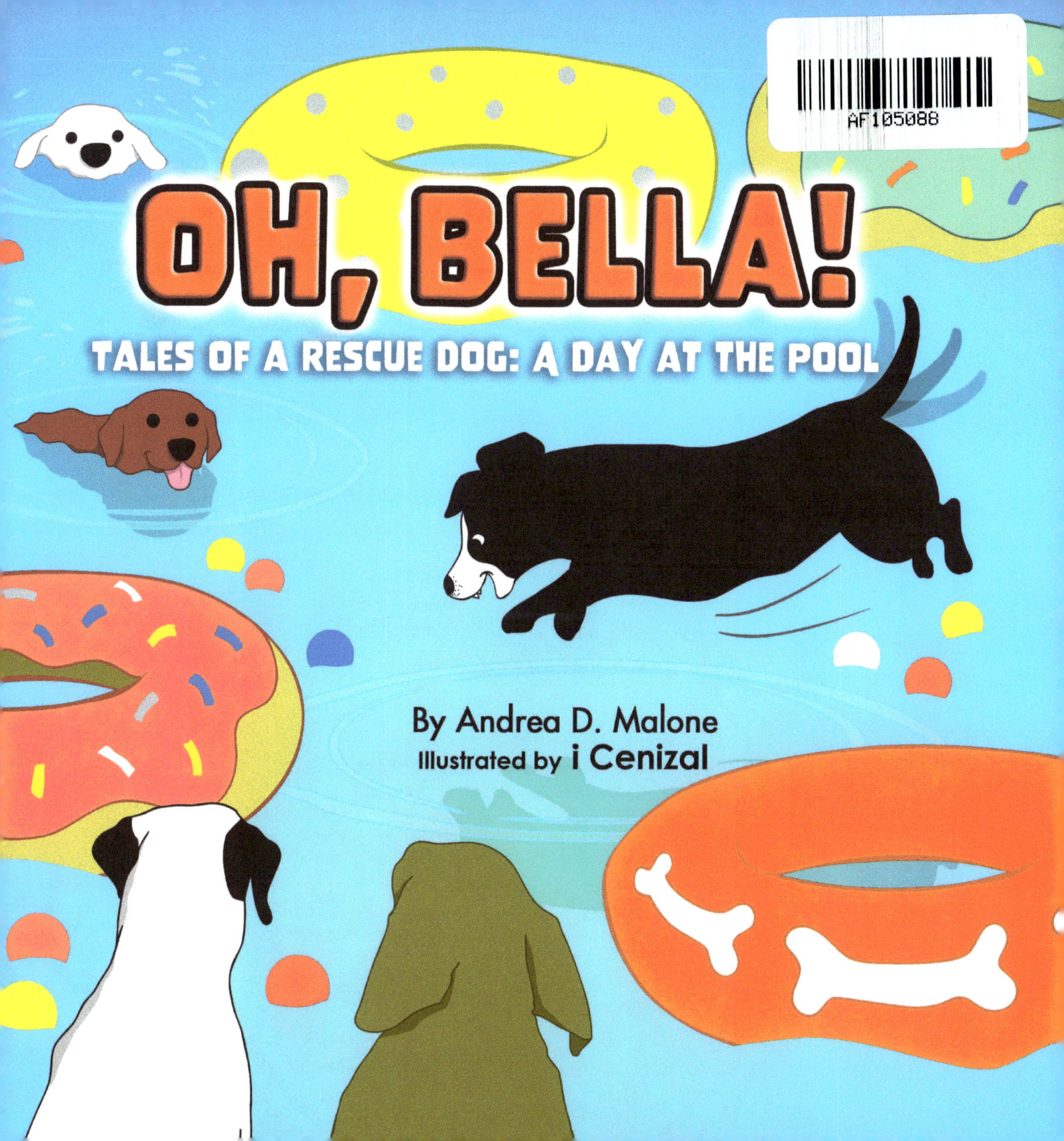

Oh, Bella! Tales of a Rescue Dog
Copyright © 2021 by Andrea D. Malone

All rights reserved. No part of this publication may be reproduced, distributed, or transmitted in any form or by any means, including photocopying, recording, or other electronic or mechanical methods, without the prior written permission of the author, except in the case of brief quotations embodied in critical reviews and certain other non-commercial uses permitted by copyright law.

tellwell

Tellwell Talent
www.tellwell.ca

ISBN
978-0-2288-3349-9 (Hardcover)
978-0-2288-3348-2 (Paperback)
978-0-2288-3350-5 (eBook)

Dedication

This story is dedicated to the memory of my aunt Duke. Aunt Duke thought my dog was very big, but she loved Bella's cuteness.

Introduction

In 2015 I adopted my Bella, a Labrador and pit bull mix, on her second birthday. I had been looking at dogs at the local animal shelter and couldn't decide which dog would be best for me. One of the workers mentioned that they had a dog that would be perfect for me and she would bring her out. At the time, I didn't know Bella was on the 24-hour euthanasia list. Bella had been at the shelter for so long! When the worker brought her out to meet me, Bella rolled over for me to give her a belly rub and we formed an instant bond. I had never been a dog owner before, and I knew in my heart I wanted to share my love with a puppy. In this series of books, I want to share my joy of Oh, Bella! Tales of a Rescue Dog.

Let's pack your bag with treats, toys, and a towel.

Oh, Bella, let's go swimming. Let's get in the truck and go bye-bye.

On our way to the swimming pool, Bella loves to put her head out the back seat window to look at the other cars as she smiles.

Oh, Bella! You're going to have so much fun swimming today - let's get our bag and go to the pool.

All the other dogs are excited to swim just like you, Bella.

Bella is having the time of her life! She runs through the pool and splashes water everywhere.

All the dogs are having a blast!

Oh, Bella, it's time to go home. We have to dry you off with your towel and make sure your ears are dry to keep your ears healthy.

While riding home from the dog park, Bella is very happy.

When Bella gets home, she is so tired she falls asleep in the doorway.

Bella is so happy after playing at the swimming pool all day. Look at my sweet baby sleeping. She is wagging her tail in her sleep. It's fun to watch Bella dream.

Meet Bella...

www.ingramcontent.com/pod-product-compliance
Lightning Source LLC
LaVergne TN
LVHW072115060526
838200LV00061B/4895